Homemade Fun

Games & Pastimes of the Early Prairies

Faye Reineberg Holt

FIFTH
HOUSE
PUBLISHERS

In 1903, this amazingly patient horse even let one child sit on its tail.

Small children love to play with pots and pans and rolling pins. In 1954, this girl, masquerading as a baker, was gleeful over the largest mincemeat pie baked by Alberta Bakeries, undoubtedly for Christmas celebrations.

A human pyramid in Smoky Lake, Alberta (c. 1927).
Provincial Archives of Alberta, Nicholas Gavinchuk Collection, G136

Play on the Prairies

Children absolutely need to play, whether it's a breathless game of tag with a gaggle of friends, a slosh through a puddle, a toss of the jacks, or an idle moment tickling their chins with foxtails growing up through the hedge. Childhood play is the training ground for an adult sense of well-being and balance, as important in the past as it is today. On the Canadian prairies long ago, children owned fewer toys, but they enjoyed amusements handed down from earlier generations and also conjured new ways to pass the time.

Today's fun is often equated with high-tech materials and gadgetry, as well as with big business. Before 1950, though, children couldn't even imagine the amazing walking, talking dolls and remote-controlled trains, cars, and airplanes of the present. They didn't plunk themselves in front of televisions, computer games, and the Internet for hours on end. In 1940, even toys of celluloid, an ancestor of modern-day plastic, were still uncommon.

Does that mean that children in "the olden days" had less fun than kids do today? Definitely not. In fact, many adults claim those childhoods of yesteryear were more fun, not less. Just like today, poverty and stress robbed some children of the time, money, or energy to be truly carefree. Nevertheless, many of those families offered strong and sup-portive environments in which childhood pleasure was somehow fostered. Kids found a million inexpensive ways to have a good time. And a few privileged children did possess all the toys and entertainments available at the time—some carried from other lands, some bought from local stores or craftspeople, and others ordered from catalogues.

No matter what their cost or origin, toys, games, and amusements varied widely in early western Canada. Some beloved games helped children to acquire skills essential to their adult

Some parents used to tell their children that babies were found in the cabbage patch. In this Manitoba patch in 1916, the kids were hard at work, but imaginative children often turned chores into games. Decades later, a doll maker and sales team made Cabbage Patch dolls popular. Provincial Archives of Manitoba, Jessop Collection 101, N3149

lives. Even if a playful venture turned out wrong, children learned about themselves, their world, and their responsibilities. Equally important, children developed feelings of self-worth and community while having a good time.

Apart from materials and technology in the two halves of the century, the biggest differences concerning play revolve around the age and definition of a child. Before the 1950s, childhood lasted only a precious few years, during which kids still had to do lots of chores important to the family's survival. With youthful enthusiasm and imagination, however, even chores could be transformed into games, and children juggled freedom and responsibility along with their work and play. By age fourteen and fifteen, many young people were encouraged to quit school and assume adult responsibilities, helping earn a living or care for family. In their mid-teens, some young people became fully responsible for their own families.

For the 1925 Boy Scout camp outside of Calgary, Alberta, these boys substituted a blanket for a trampoline, and somehow tossed one daring scout high in the air.
Glenbow Archives PA2318–237

Church and farmers' picnics and sports days included a wide range of races. In 1932, these boys from College Mathieu, a school in Gravelbourg, Saskatchewan, are preparing for the gunny sack race, not open to girls. Saskatchewan Archives Board R–A 19819

In 1967, these children discovered an inventive way of making cans into stilts. Glenbow Archives, Calgary Herald *Collection, Children, File 3, 2 June 1967*

Children of Two Worlds

Before settlers arrived from around the world, Native children played with toys and games fashioned from the horns and bones of buffalo, elk, and deer. Toys were whittled from wood and sewn from hide and sinew. Feathers became decorations, and stones found their way into play. Most games and amusements taught essential skills. Many of the pastimes could be played all year round, but a few Native inventions, such as snowshoe races and sledding, were seasonal sports.

Long before the children of settlers took sleds and toboggans to frozen rivers and snow-covered hills, Native children enjoyed sliding on snow. In fact, the French and English words for "toboggan" are rooted in the Algonquian language. Native children's sled runners were made from the ribs of wild animals, such as buffalo, and tied on with rawhide. The seat was also made of hide. Each end of the sled had a willow cross-bar. Rawhide rope was tied to the front for steering and pulling, and sometimes the sleds were decorated with buffalo tails. If necessary, a long piece of bark substituted for a toboggan. There were many tobogganing games. Sometimes the boys

On 23 December 1919, at River Park in Winnipeg, the wooden toboggan run was steep and impressive. Enjoying this toboggan party are young newspaper carriers for the Manitoba Free Press.

Provincial Archives of Manitoba, L.B. Foote Collection 1229, N2205 became hunters, while the girls acted the part of the prey, the buffalo. Each time a boy caught a girl, he counted a kill.

Children played with tops made of bone, horn, and wood, and even in winter, they spun their tops on ice and snow. Native children also enjoyed ring-and-pin games, in which hollow bone segments were thrown into the air and caught on a needle. These games had complex rules for scoring points, as did hoop games, and the bow-and-arrow competitions.

Most boys' games were competitive and developed natural abilities, such as hand-eye coordination. Boys loved war scenarios, too, and if one child pretended to be shot, another would assume the role of the medicine man, squeezing herbal medicines onto pretend wounds.

For Native girls, most play trained them for grown-up responsibilities. Mothers and grandmothers made dolls, miniature cradle-boards, boxes, and travois for them. Both girls and boys received finely whittled horses. They also enjoyed races and acrobatics on real horses, which were prized animals.

Storytelling served two practical functions: to entertain children and to pass the culture to a new generation. Then along came the European and Canadian missionaries, who told very different stories and discounted tales about the god of Thunder and spoke of a Christ child born in a stable. They told of miracles and of sin. They also disapproved of Native war games and gambling amusements.[1]

As missionaries, fur-traders, North-West Mounted Police, and settlers arrived in the Northwest, they added new elements to play. Métis children inherited ideas from their Native parent and from their white parent, generally English, Scottish, or French. A few Métis boys whose parents were wealthy were sent to school in eastern Canada or Britain and thrown into the world of cricket, tennis, and badminton. Throughout Canada, snow-sliding games became popular with all children. Games made from bone and horn were replaced by similar games made of new material, and bow-and-arrow and medicine-wheel games began to disappear.

Children of early prairie settlers amused themselves with their surroundings and discarded household items. In the spring of 1884, Rev. Leonard Gaetz and his family left Ontario and eventually settled in the fledgling community of Red Deer, Alberta. His son, Linton, was never bored there:

Burrowing into snowdrifts, connecting one den with another, then caving it all in before someone else did—this was fun. Wind-packed snow crusts, stacked, made forts. Behind these, ammunition was hastily made and bombardment to and from lasted till someone was hurt or one little group ran off having had enough.

Linton loved to run with his siblings and friends, and a hoop at his side heightened the thrills. "You searched for a wheel from a cast-off baby carriage or some such contraption, found a stick to which you nailed a crosspiece and [pushing the hoop with it] you were all hot to trot with your pals, preferably on a wood sidewalk where your feet and heels made gentle music hour after hour, day after day."[2]

The Gaetz children tunnelled into the hay, filling their hair and clothes with dust and hay to satisfy "some primordial

At Gleichen, Alberta, during the early 1920s, Campbell Brown (left, holding tire) and his friends rolled around, not on tires but in them. The inner tubes of tires were great fun at the swimming hole, too. Glenbow Archives 336–13

In 1916, these Manitoba boys stacked oats, while the girls appear to have brought lunch. The work was real, but playing in hay and straw stacks could also be a lot of fun. Provincial Archives of Manitoba, Jessop Collection 188

instinct." So did Georgina Thomson and her sister. These city children from eastern Canada moved to a homestead near Nanton, Alberta, in the early 1900s. The girls did chores and helped put up hay, but "we thought this fun, not work, and loved to play in the dry, sun-cured hay in spite of the spear grass."[3]

For the girls, the wildflowers of the prairies were fascinating. With their dog, they wandered on old buffalo trails so the sharp seed pods of spear grass wouldn't stick to their legs. As they walked, they made up names for wildflowers they couldn't identify. One, the duck-bill, was really a shooting star.

Not Long Ago

It didn't take much to keep kids out of mischief. Give children an old can, and they'd come home late for supper because they were playing kick the can. They counted how many times they could make flat rocks skip over the surface of sloughs and lakes. Using a slate and chalk, or else paper and pencil, they drew masterpieces or enjoyed games of hangman, tic-tac-toe, and squares, dots, and triangles. With scissors, they would transform paper into paper-chain jewelry, airplanes, hats, fans, or pin-the-tail-on-the-donkey. They could fold a piece of paper into a frog or into a wonderful finger game that would foretell the future.

Wooden Tinkertoys kept boys and girls busy for hours. Steel Meccano sets were also popular with boys. South Saskatchewan Photo Museum

Paper was surprisingly precious. Even newspapers were often too valuable to be used for fun. They were needed for papering the walls of prairie homes to keep out drafts. So paper crafts were limited. Some children, such as those in the James Caswell family who lived near Moose Jaw, Saskatchewan, in 1887, made Christmas cards for friends and relatives, and other children made paper chains and snowflakes as Christmas decorations. When families were poor, however, even that was too impractical.

Girls were encouraged to embroider and crochet tea towels and pillowcases. They knitted and wove, and they twisted rag ropes for Mother's rugs or pot holders. Older girls made rag dolls for themselves or younger siblings, and in doing so, they created treasures and learned valuable skills.

Most crafts were based on common things, and on most farms—even in the Thirties—there were potatoes. Potato printing was a fine activity for a rainy or snowy day. Some children were fortunate enough to use watercolour paints or ink. Others might use berry juice from raspberries or saskatoons. Children also carved soap for print-making, but soap was precious— either expensive to buy or tedious to make. Fortunately, some mothers were willing to use soap chips for laundry or dishes. For children, leftover soap chips could mean fun. Most children loved to blow bubbles and some invented unique bubble blowers. One young Saskatchewan girl in the 1950s cut an onion stalk into a tube. Then she stood on a chair by the kitchen sink creating one glittering, magical sphere after another.

In poor families, other common commodities, such as flour and cornstarch, were too valuable to be squandered on playdough.

Rowing a boat and balancing on a log were fun. Equally fun for many farm children was balancing on rolling, empty barrels.
City of Edmonton Archives EA 63–216

Instead, children kneaded real bread dough and cut cookie dough into shapes. In families that could spare enough flour to make glue, children used old catalogues or newspapers to decorate homemade toys, boxes, or boards.

Capable older children sometimes built kites from string and paper or cloth. A very lucky few received costly leather, copper, or woodworking tools. Mostly, such tools belonged to fathers or adult brothers, who might use them to make toys for young children.

Girls, especially, loved to skip. With a skipping rope, a girl could jump and chant, learning whether she would marry a tinker, tailor, soldier, sailor, rich man, poor man, beggar man, thief, doctor, lawyer, or Indian chief. Skipping ropes and rhymes went together like salt and "pepper," a word that made children skip at a furious pace! A skipper would duck in under the rope, and a chant would begin: "Teddy bear, teddy bear, turn around; teddy bear, teddy bear, touch the ground." Skipping chants and songs abounded.

Boys spent hours playing cops and robbers or cowboys and Indians. Not that they necessarily knew anything about actual Native people. Instead, they gleaned their ideas from American books and, much later, American movies. Early in the 1900s, boys like Wallace Stegner, who grew up at Wood Mountain near the Alberta-Saskatchewan border, learned about Indians from *The Last of the Mohicans*. He and other curious boys tried to lurk around Native camps about once a year, running for dear life if they were approached by anyone from the camp. Relationships between Natives and settlers were not always warm and friendly, so white children's notions of Native life were usually

These Calgary Boy Scouts were building birdhouses in about 1924. Children more often learned the craft by trial and error or under the tutelage of fathers or older brothers. Glenbow Archives NA 4487–3

limited to sticking a feather into a homemade headband, and using twigs for a bow and arrows.

Playing cowboy and riding a hobby horse fashioned from a branch or broom handle became a timeless favourite pastime for most boys. Samuel Hofer recalled his childhood fascination with cowboys in his 1991 book *Born Hutterite*. Growing up on the Rockyview Colony in the Alberta foothills,

he fancied himself the Cowboy Kid, riding off to stop drunken outlaws from robbing a bank. He really wanted orange pop as a reward, but the cowboys of his imagination were tough, drank beer, and played poker, or else they ate beans and drank cowboy coffee at cactus-burning campfires. In fact, the "let's pretend" adventures of prairie children were filled with such stereotypes from the early settlement days until the 1960s, and play was seldom censored by the real world of adults.

For cowboys and Indians, this 1920s group was very imaginative about interpreting Native dress. Kids also loved dressing as cowboys or cowgirls. Boys usually wanted "real" toy guns and swords but sometimes a pointed finger had to do. Saskatchewan Archives Board R-B 11362–2

In this 1937 picture, Joan Munton reads to her doll. By then books
for children were becoming more common in prairie homes.
Provincial Archives of Manitoba, Frank Munton Collection 6.25.26

Mail-order Toys

Very fortunate children owned manufactured toys. Settlers had little space for playthings when they packed essentials for the journey to the homestead. They might be able to afford some manufactured toys later on, but the local general store carried only a tiny selection. In contrast, you could buy almost anything you could think of through the mail.

By 1901, the T. Eaton Company advertised Eaton's Beauty dolls. Prices ranged from one to six dollars. Tiny dolls, called kewpie dolls, were more affordable. Attached to little canes, they were often sold at rodeos and fairs. Glenbow Library, T. Eaton Company Catalogue, Fall and Winter, 1922–1923, 357

By 1888–1889, the list of toys was extensive in the Eaton's catalogue—for those who could afford them.

Wealthy parents might buy miniature farms and stables, or perhaps toy soldiers, doll cradles, and toy stoves. For twenty cents to $1.50, a child could have her own little tea set. Toy guns cost ten to ninety cents, and toy swords were ten to fifty cents. If money was no object, a child might find a toy train, steamship, dump cart, paintbox, toy piano, or music box on Christmas morning. Dolls came in all shapes, colours, and sizes, ranging in price from three pennies to $3.85.

In the late 1800s, catalogues carried only a few drawings of home and farm merchandise—no bright photographs in a toy section. So the catalogue was not yet the dream book that children would gaze at in years to come. Children and parents alike, though, did peruse the catalogue in the outhouse before ripping off a page or two for toilet paper.

The 1902 Sears, Roebuck, and Company catalogue featured a Ouija board, but one of the most popular items was a reversible board featuring fifty-one games, including checkers, backgammon, crokinole, billiards, three-ring, and pin pool. The board came with rings, cues, pins, and other components, and cost just under two dollars. For those on a strict budget, dominoes cost only a nickel.

By 1910, catalogues carried kaleidoscopes, musical tops, drawing slates, and jack-in-the-boxes. The Hudson's Bay catalogue advertised a generous array of toy animals. There were stuffed, wooden, and celluloid animals, covered with wool, fur, felt, and "plush," as well as cloth-covered ducks and roosters with feather tails.

A large toy, such as a croquet set, Noah's ark filled with animals, wagon, toboggan, or rocking horse, would command a higher price. What struggling family in 1901 could buy a rocking horse for three to eighteen dollars, when a child's bed cost three to seven dollars?

In the early 1900s, toys didn't make particularly sophisticated sounds. Today's toys speak or sing clearly, or walkie-talkies and tape recorders allow the child to speak. A toy of old might squeak if squeezed or say a few garbled words if a string was pulled. A music box, when wound up, could creak out a pretty tune. But a child who wanted words would have to sit by an early radio or look at a book.

Catalogues offered books, some especially for children. Reading was an indulgence in many families, not a necessity. But if the family could afford the books—and the kerosene—the children could spend long winter nights reading by lamplight.

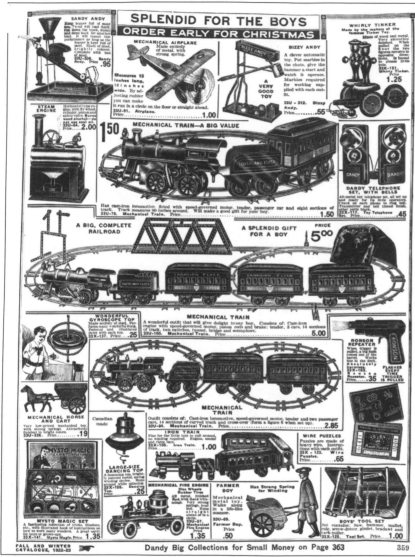

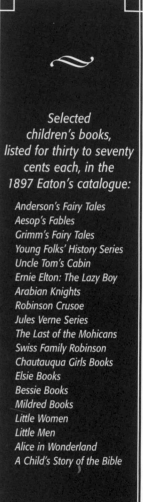
Dandy Big Collections for Small Money on Page 363

*Transportation themes fascinated most boys. This catalogue also advertised wagons, boys'
three-wheeled velocipedes (tricycles), a pedi-car (tricycles for tots), rocking horses, sleds, and a
toy car.* Glenbow Library, Trade Catalogues, T. Eaton and Co., Fall and Winter Catalogue, 1922–1923, 359

Only Happyland Beats Mischief

In new towns such as early Winnipeg, the streets were muddy, especially during the spring flood season, so wooden sidewalks were built to keep the pedestrians out of the muck. When the ground dried up, children congregated in the crawl space under the sidewalk. The sons of James Scott secreted themselves there for hours, entertained by those strolling overhead. They'd gleefully stick willow branches up between the sidewalk boards, causing passersby to stumble. If a female victim's male escort chased the boys out, the ensuing race only added to the fun.

Children also loved to pilfer ice from the door-to-door ice wagon. In Winnipeg, Al Tassie and his friends waited until the ice man made a delivery to a back door. Then they scurried off with slivers and baseball-sized chunks of ice, sucking on them and bragging about close escapes. If a girl wandered along, daring to intrude on their group, one daredevil boy would hold her while another would drop ice down the back of her shirt.

On summer evenings before the First World War, boys bicycled or walked to the Minto Armouries and watched real soldiers drill with real machine guns and bayonets. The boys wandered into the buildings, soaking up the smell of grease and leather. On the way home, they boasted about their favourite regiment and argued over who was best: the Winnipeg Grenadiers, Fort Garrys, Cameron Highlanders, or Strathcona Horse.

Kids could never resist a body of water, whether it was a creek or a lake, and if it was big enough, they loved to build rafts. In the first half of the century, children gathered driftwood, cast-off boards, and abandoned railway ties for rafts, sailing them along water-filled ditches and across sloughs. Near Winnipeg Beach, culverts and roads provided obstacles and also reasonably safe boundaries. Sometimes

concerned parents forbade rafting and meted out punishment when their children came home soaked after an upset.

Children also created their own drainage ditches and rivers, from tiny water lanes carved with a branch, to large diversions dug with a spade. They launched miniature sailboats and ships that were wonders of design, hand-carved from kindling wood or folded from paper. When the prized possession sank or floated away, a child had an excuse to craft another one, even better than the last.

Ruth and Gordon Waterhouse dressed as Red Cross workers for a 1929 chautauqua parade. Children loved dressing in costumes and decorating their bikes and wagons.
Glenbow Archives NA 2056–8

By 1907 in Winnipeg, children discovered a more sophisticated kind of magic at a place called Happyland, "The City of Fun for Old and Young." There, on summer days, children visited circus tents, watched aerialists and diving ponies, and skated at the roller rink. A figure-eight rollercoaster provided thrills, and a ride on the Ferris wheel offered a breathtaking view of the city. Ladies and children didn't need a male escort to protect them, and when the circus moved on, children could search the grass for pennies.

Most larger communities attracted chautauquas (programs of music, theatre, and lectures), exhibitions, or fairs. Slowly, zoos began to appear in the West, and the Calgary Stampede became a popular mecca for local children. Eventually, rodeos featured child contestants riding calves and displaying their skills—not as pretend cowpokes, but as real cowboys.

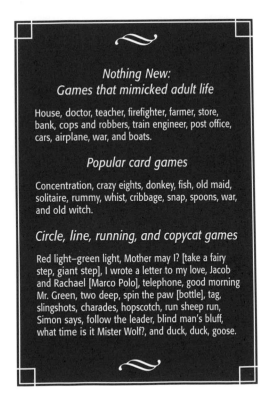

Nothing New:
Games that mimicked adult life

House, doctor, teacher, firefighter, farmer, store, bank, cops and robbers, train engineer, post office, cars, airplane, war, and boats.

Popular card games

Concentration, crazy eights, donkey, fish, old maid, solitaire, rummy, whist, cribbage, snap, spoons, war, and old witch.

Circle, line, running, and copycat games

Red light–green light, Mother may I? [take a fairy step, giant step], I wrote a letter to my love, Jacob and Rachael [Marco Polo], telephone, good morning Mr. Green, two deep, spin the paw [bottle], tag, slingshots, charades, hopscotch, run sheep run, Simon says, follow the leader, blind man's bluff, what time is it Mister Wolf?, and duck, duck, goose.

Animal Playmates

Wild animals were endlessly interesting to children. Marie Albina Hamilton was only four when she moved with her father and mother to Regina, Saskatchewan, in 1882. Regina, at that time, was basically a tent town. Few buffalo were left on the plains, but her older brother found a buffalo cow near a surveyors' camp and brought it home. He penned the animal near the family's store. To the young girl, the buffalo was fascinating, but it was not an animal to pet and tame. So with childhood curiosity, she poked sticks

Clearly, Beatrice Benson of Munson, Alberta, trained her dog successfully. Children also tried to train horses, rabbits, and frogs. Some had pet salamanders, snakes, beaver, and deer. Glenbow Archives NA 2543–14

through the bars at it, until finally it rushed at her and frightened her.

One afternoon in about 1885, the daughters of Englishman Henry Fisher, who had newly settled near Regina, were invited to afternoon tea at Government House. On the way, the youngest spied a lost kitten on the prairie. Her sister stopped the buggy, and the little girl soon snuggled the waif in her shawl. At tea, a strong smell permeated Government House. The servants and other visitors were not at all hospitable, and the girls felt nauseated. To break the uncomfortable tension, the little girl opened her shawl to show everyone her new pet. Despite his laughter, the governor remained polite. The lost kitten was a baby skunk, an animal that would frequently fascinate and perfume prairie children and their dogs.

In 1910, when Edwart Coutts was eleven years old, he received a pup from his father, who was the Baptist minister at Carman, Manitoba. Although it was a mongrel, Edwart named it Collie, and the dog brought

When there wasn't a real horse to ride, kids devised imaginative substitutes. This one is better than most.
Harold Unsworth photo, John Charyk Collection, Charyk family

Edwart immeasurable pleasure. Training was challenging, but soon Collie could pull a sled. By slowly increasing the weight on the sled, eventually Edwart's pet could pull him on a toboggan.

Collie was not perfect in every way. Like other dogs, it always rose to a fight, but Edwart and his friends discovered that shaking pepper on the dogs' noses curtailed hostilities. While the dogs sneezed, the boys would pull them apart. One winter, the boys decided to make their four "sleigh dogs" into a dogsled team. When all the dogs were hitched in tandem, one boy shouted, "Mush!" The lead dog turned, and soon all the dogs were in an uproar. Separating them was an ordeal, and that was the end of the boyhood chums' dog-team dream.

Horses were best friends to many children, but usually were too busy to play. Out of necessity, most children rode and learned to drive horses hitched to farm implements, cutters, wagons, and carriages. Sometimes childhood chores included caring for horses, which were good listeners and, if well-trained, were endlessly patient with child riders. Even stubborn, wild, or mean-spirited horses drew pint-sized cowboys and cowgirls to them like magnets. A few children rode to school on horseback, and the luckiest of all actually had a horse to call their own. Mostly, horses and horse books were the stuff of dreams and daydreams. In fact, that was another fine pastime. While lying on the grass, an imaginative child could picture all sorts of creatures racing and rambling amongst the billowing cumulus clouds.

When it came to hopping on a real-life pet or domestic animal, farm children would ride anything with four legs and half their size. It remained timeless fun. Even in the early 1960s, one Saskatchewan tot from the Saskatoon area was not deterred by the fact that turkeys had two legs. Why should that stop her? Before she knew it, she and the turkey were off and running. The feat required bravery, too. Some farm children considered turkeys the most ugly, disdainful, egotistical, ill-tempered, and threatening beasts in the farmyard playground, and definitely a creature for nightmares. Was the young girl dared by a mischievous brother nine years her senior? Did he think it would be a hoot to watch her tame a turkey? Like many childhood experiences, the memory of the ride lives on, but the reason for it has faded.

To Bert Hoskin of Carstairs, Alberta, pigs were for riding. Many farm children also rode sheep, cows, calves, and other creatures. Glenbow Archives NA 4182–15

Better than Store-bought

Millicent Banner Hansen grew up near Birtle, Manitoba, where she, her siblings, friends, and cousins enjoyed dozens of outdoor games, including complex variations of hide-and-seek. Sometimes, the hiders had a leader who followed the seekers and called out colour-coded hints about safety and danger. Because there were so many placcs to hide on the farm, a hider might draw a map in the dirt to help the seekers. The children also loved to jump from the rafters into the hay in the barn's loft.

This teeter-totter, near Prince Albert, Saskatchewan, was simply made from a long plank placed over a sawhorse. Saskatchewan Archives Board R–A 1769

Millicent's father could make playthings out of, say, a few old pieces of lumber, some spikes, or leather. Handy with wood and tools, he made a swing, a teeter-totter, and stilts, but he fashioned far more elaborate amusements, too. When the children were nearly old enough for school, he made them a cart. For it, he built a box and then attached binder wheels, which were fastened to a wooden axle. Using a tree stump a metre (about three feet) high as the base and attaching a plank, he made a merry-go-round. One child straddled each end of the plank, and a third child pushed them round and round.

These children have a very fancy tea party. Others made do with wooden boxes for furnishings, leaves as plates, and cans as imaginary cups and saucers.
Provincial Archives of Manitoba, Martha Knapp Collection 31, N17375

The Banner girls were equally adept at discovering creative solutions to meet their needs. When they wanted a playhouse, they found an empty shed or tramped out a square in the bushes. Then they used whatever they could find to make the house a home. Sometimes, they walled off an area with old sheets; wooden boxes made chairs and tables. The girls didn't have a children's tea set and didn't serve tea, but they did serve their own special brand of coffee, made from brown dock seeds. And they made better mud pies than most girls did: "We borrowed eggs and then mixed them with dirt."

Millicent and her twin sister, Connie, who dressed alike, spent hours cutting out new clothes from the catalogue for their cardboard and paper dolls. They ignored the catalogue's household possessions. "We were more into fashion."

They never had birthday parties. Nor did they have a Christmas tree until the late 1930s. Each child received a single gift at Christmas. One year, the girls received brooches. Another year, their mother made them dresses. The gifts were always "necessities, not something we wanted," and the children always knew beforehand what their gift was because they went "snooping."

To her, during those years, families were definitely closer. "Those were our playmates. You couldn't sit down and watch a television show and shut out the world. We were interacting all the time."

In the long summer evenings, after a hot day, the Banner children would play tag or just roughhouse, and they loved it. "We were never bored," and the good times did not require a myriad of possessions. Despite having grown up during the Depression, "I remember my childhood as being exceedingly happy," she recalls.[4]

On Christmas 1904, Santa found the Bow River Horse Ranch near Cochrane, Alberta. With two drums under the tree, the parents of Victor (left) and Everette Goddard were likely to need earplugs.
Glenbow Archives NA 2084–37

In Saskatchewan, the Young family had five girls, all older than their baby brother, Bob. Audrey Young Smith and Edith Young Vereshagin spent their early years on a farm near Moosomin, and their play closely paralleled real families and relationships. Even if it was fun, not every moment was glorious.

As a tiny girl, hide-and-seek frustrated Edith. "I could never get home. I would have to be 'It' over and over, until somebody would take pity on me." When playing house, if the younger girls, Edith and Grace, were the children, the pretend home was a happy one "because we would obey our pretend parents [May and Audrey]." Once, they switched roles, and May and Audrey did not obey their pretend parents. "They were bad. They got into mischief. We could not control them. It was very frustrating. We never tried that again."

During the 1930s, the family moved to Carrot River, Saskatchewan. Before settling on a homestead, the Youngs shared a house with another family. Now the six Young children had two more playmates, twelve-year-old Jean and eight-year-old Lynn. They had built a small treehouse and were adding a second storey. "One fall day, while Jean and Lynn were at school, Grace and I [Edith] decided to surprise them and finish the house. We were perched up on the first floor, hammering away at the second floor when suddenly, kerplunk." They and the floor fell to the ground, and the treehouse was never finished.

While still living with Jean and Lynn, the children also played house in a granary. They made cookies, which Jean called "kisses," from snow and ashes. When the Youngs moved again, they had a nearby slough. Like adult homesteaders, the girls made their playhouse from available materials:

> *We girls made little huts from willows. We'd put moss in the cracks to finish them. The huts were big enough for about three of us to crawl in. We'd read there on hot summer days. Our brother Bob made a raft, which he used to float on the slough. A little peninsula jutted out into the slough. Grace and I were standing there one day. At one point, I sneaked up behind her. She was supposed to guess whom it was, but she struggled to be free. I held on, keeping her eyes covered. Suddenly, we both fell backwards into the water. What a surprise for both of us, but I guess we deserved it.* [5]

Very few days were too cold for young hockey enthusiasts, and James Gray was one of them. Born in 1906, he spent his childhood in Winnipeg. His first skates were hand-me down bob skates, which were clamped and strapped tightly to his boots. Eventually, he graduated to new hand-me-downs that were screwed to a pair of well-worn boots for the entire winter. Finally, at fourteen, he acquired hockey skates, which were the latest rage and had regular blades fixed to hockey boots.

Like most kids, he learned to skate on sloughs and in flooded backyards. There, James and his friends scored goals, and on bitter days, they warmed up in old woodsheds. As they grew older, larger and better rinks beckoned. At the Kennedy rink, owned and oper-

In about 1921, Walter and Norman Chubb of Bon Accord, Alberta, had a stick and puck ready for hockey. In poor families, boots, balls, tin cans, or frozen cow-pies became adequate substitutes for a real puck. Glenbow Archives NA 2041–2

ated by the two Wilkinson brothers, the entry fee was ten cents per child.

Fortunately for the boys, and unfortunately for the Wilkinsons, the property wasn't easily fenced. The skaters didn't really need a shack. Some left home in their skates, while others abandoned their footwear for skates on the nearby riverbank. Presto! They were on the rink, passing pucks—and it didn't cost a dime.

Wielding hockey sticks, the Wilkinsons policed the freeloading boys. The warm-up shack was easily controlled. There, one brother sold drinks, laces, and admissions. On bitterly cold days, the brazen freeloaders were even more brazen, but once the hockey players were in the shack, the Wilkinsons had them. While the boys warmed up, the Wilkinson brothers might confiscate hockey sticks or the footwear on the riverbank. Only when admission money was paid did the skaters recover their belongings.

For countless prairie boys, such as Saskatchewan's Gordie Howe, hockey was more than a way to pass the long winter hours. It was a passion, and Howe became a superstar in the National Hockey League. By the time Wayne Gretzky, the Great One, was breaking hockey records, parents were buying children good skates, knee pads, elbow pads, helmets, and visors to help them play well and be safe. Yet as a child, Gretzky had studied the moves of Howe for inspiration, and Howe had first played hockey with very basic equipment and skates on the outdoor ice of his prairie home.

Henry (Nibs) Akers was born in southern Alberta in 1919 and grew up in Medicine Hat, Alberta. His three older brothers, Bill, Fred, and Frank, helped create a world of play for Nibs and other children.

In the dry belt surrounding Medicine Hat, there were few sloughs for swimming. The nearest lake was Elk Water Lake, about sixty-one kilometres (thirty-eight miles) away at a time when few families had cars. Kids swam in the quiet spots along rivers. Determined and willing workers, Nib's older brothers and their friends had a better plan.

They set to work damming an area of Wales Creek, about eight kilometres (five miles) from home. Sixteen to eighteen years old, they cleared out the side of the creek, widened the creek bed, and created a top-notch swimming hole. The finished dam filled with water, and where the swimming hole was deep enough, they added a plank diving board. There, on hot summer days, as many as twenty-five kids gathered to keep cool, splashing, diving, and swimming.

Most were boys, and with two exceptions, age was no barrier. Swimmers had to be old enough to get themselves to the swimming hole, and adults were not particularly welcome. With bicycles, the distance was not a huge obstacle, but one long hill slowed their progress. Unbeknownst to their parents, some boys wandered to the CPR railyards and furtively hitched a ride. Since the hill was steep, freight trains travelled very slowly on the way up. Once at the top of the hill, the boys jumped off and walked, still fresh for the day's good times. At day's end, trudging home was the only option since the trains travelled downhill far too fast to risk a ride.

During each of two summers, Henry, his brother Frank, and a friend camped at the nearby swimming hole for a week. During the winter, the swimming hole became a skating rink. Henry's brothers and friends built a toboggan run and a warm-up shack. They installed a pot-bellied stove and took

While kids could skinny-dip at swimming holes, most pre-1930 public swimming pools required boys and men to wear swimsuits that covered their chest, shoulders, and torso.
South Saskatchewan Photo Museum

turns gathering coal that spilled from wagons.

Nibs and his friends were also lured to the Dreamland Theatre. On Saturday mornings, they headed to the local Chinese market gardener and spent two or three hours pulling weeds in the onion patch, earning a nickel an hour. In the afternoon, they paid their way into the wonderland of the silver screen and spent a few cents on candy.

At about seven, Nibs acquired his first bicycle, a hand-me-down. By ten, he wanted a new bike, so he sold the *Calgary Herald* at a nickel apiece on the street. For every two papers, he earned a nickel, but bicycles cost about twenty dollars. Eventually, Nibs and his father hammered out a deal with a local merchant: Nibs paid five dollars down and settled the rest at about a dollar a week. Finally, he had his new bicycle.[6]

When camping with family, friends, Boy Scouts, or Girl Guides, most children enjoyed cooking over an open fire. Provincial Archives of Alberta O.M.I. OB 6167

Games, Races, and Gopher Tails

Born in 1929 and growing up near Brownfield, Alberta, Ellen Cole Biette was a child of the difficult Thirties. Her mother died soon after Ellen was born, and without siblings, she spent hours as a small child entertaining herself. Not one to let solitude be an insurmountable obstacle to fun, she played a version of anti-I-over—by herself. Usually played by two teams, one person would throw the ball over a roof to the other team. Whoever caught it ran like the wind around the building and tagged as many opponents as possible. Tagged opponents were then on the ball carrier's team. Many children never got

By 1921, some community playgrounds had slides, teeter-totters, swings, and other gymnastic equipment. Glenbow Archives NA 3766–51

the ball over the roof until they were twelve, but young Ellen wasn't thwarted by the challenges. She heaved the ball over the roof and raced to the other side to catch it. Other times, she expected her dog to catch the ball, so she could throw it once more.

Then there was an old witch game, which may have been invented by a playmate. Opposite corners outside the school were designated as homes for the witch and the mother. Mother ran to the witch's house, yelling, "Your fence is broken! Your cows are out!" Coming to fetch their mother, the children cried, "The kettle's boiling over!" While Mother hurried home, the witch caught the children, imprisoned them, and cast a spell—or at least named them fruits, flowers, or vegetables. When Mother came to reclaim her children, she had to guess who was what, or else her poor children remained in the witch's power.

Children also became fruits in upset-the-fruit-basket, which resembled musical chairs. The children outnumbered the desks or chairs by one, and "It" might command peaches and pears to switch seats. Mayhem occurred when "It" called, "Upset the fruit basket!" Then peaches, pears, apples, bananas, oranges, raspberries, strawberries, and saskatoons would jump from their seats, scrambling for another, because the person without a desk or chair became "It."

In one game, "It" was a scholar. Rural schools had huge, rolled maps above the blackboard. "It" would glance casually at the map and choose a place, and the other children would guess the location. Remaining "It" was desirable, and good scholars could focus on little-known places. Did children change the city or country when a playmate guessed correctly? Undoubtedly, some had their suspicions!

Ellen played other games based on cooperation. In tug-of-war and Red Rover, the strongest team, not the strongest individual, won. Steal sticks, sometimes called prisoner's base, also required teamwork, plus wood from the woodpile. Children gathered an equal number of sticks for each team and placed them behind their team lines. No man's land lay between the two lines. A nearby but separate area was prison. If you stayed on your "property," you were safe. But safe wasn't fun, and chaos soon reigned supreme. Players from one team would run to steal wood from the other team. If caught, they were taken to prison. A teammate could either rescue a prisoner or steal a stick—but not both. During the rescue, both the rescuer and prisoner might be caught, and then both went to prison. Each child could play offence or defence at will.

Many children spent summer holidays at camp or Vacation Bible School, where they made crafts, learned songs, and played games. At Victoria Park in Regina, Saskatchewan, these "summer students" played London Bridge.

Saskatchewan Archives Board R–A 8346–2

friends played a popular variation of two deep. Boys formed an outside circle, and girls formed an inside circle. A male "It" would wink at a girl, and the boy standing behind her would try to keep her from running after "It." In those days, girls didn't run with or after boys. The flirtation "was fun, a teenage thing," and undoubtedly especially fun for those who were shy or whose parents were very strict.[7]

Kids from six to sixteen often played and shared good

Only the most daring and speedy children could steal a stick, take it home, rescue a prisoner, take him or her home, catch thieves, and take them to prison—all without getting caught. When everyone from one team was in prison, the game was over. However, with dozens of children playing, the game could go on forever—or at least until recess or lunch break ended.

By age twelve, Ellen and her

Children of all ages used to play together, and here the children of the Spring Lake School District in Saskatchewan are shown building a snowman, c. 1920.

Saskatchewan Archives Board R–A 20888

times together. Being older and stronger meant more responsibility, but older children were also favourites for captain. They could show off a little—if so inclined. To bully was another thing, and in small communities and schools, a bad reputation was tricky to escape.

Play involved other clear, unwritten rules regarding behaviour, too. Older children were expected to allow younger children a chance to excel. Marjorie Dyer Kross was born in 1911 near Carlyle, Saskatchewan, where her parents homesteaded. She loved to run and was good at it. At church picnics, she regularly won a nickel or dime in foot races. "That was big money in those days." Because contestants were few, their age, ability, and size varied. For one race, Marjorie was confident she could once again win the nickel. The children lined up, with Marjorie beside the starter. "Go!" signalled the starter, and Marjorie leapt forward. The starter held her back. Once he released her, Marjorie ran hard. Suddenly, she stumbled in a gopher hole and fell. She didn't win the nickel that day. "I was so mad," she recalls, "I cried." [8]

Marjorie remembers cheating as a serious transgression. For instance, prairie children loved fox and geese after a fresh snowfall. They tramped out a huge circle in the snow and made paths to the centre, which was home and safe. Along the outer circle, the fox lurked, waiting to catch daring geese who inevitably tempted fate and the fox by leaving home. Suddenly, they were vulnerable. If the fox came close, some geese cut corners back to the centre, "and we weren't supposed to. We were supposed to follow the lines."

Most children shared what little they

For Halloween in 1933, these Alberta children were dressed to impress or scare. Older town-children were far more likely to go trick-or-treating than rural children, who would have to walk far to knock on a neighbour's door. A common prank was upsetting outhouses. City of Edmonton Archives EA 160–530

had, and they innovated or made do when necessary. The school had no ball, so the Dyer children took their rubber ball. There was no bat, so players simply used their hands as bats. Marjorie loved reading, but the Dyer family and the school library had few books. So she read and reread *Little Lucy's Wonderful Globe*.

At her rural school, there was no Halloween party, just a Valentine's Day party for which the children made valentines to exchange and the parents made cookies. Elsewhere, some children may have bobbed for apples, but not so at Marjorie's school.

Her only concert was not a Christmas concert. When Marjorie was in about grade eight, the teacher staged a concert at the church to raise money for a school organ. The children donned black-stocking masks and sang "Old Black Joe," "My Old Kentucky Home," and "Swing Low Sweet Chariot." They were a big hit, raising forty dollars for the organ. A play based on African American themes, *Uncle Tom's Cabin*, was also performed at church, this time by a travelling group.

These real children were the imaginary children of The Old Woman Who Lived in a Shoe. During 1923, in Winnipeg, they dramatized the popular nursery rhyme.
Red Deer Museum, Florence Cottingham Collection

Although African American settlers lived near Edmonton, Alberta, few prairie kids ever saw a black person. Still, the Dyer girls had Aunt Jemima and Uncle Tom dolls. Marjorie thinks the dolls may have been bought, with money or coupons, from the Aunt Jemima Pancake Flour Company.

The Dyer girls had other dolls, too, and many doll clothes, which their mother sewed after finishing those for her nine children. Their father built doll cradles. As well, he nailed a cross-bar to a stick and showed them how to roll an upright hoop, usually an old wheel from a child's wagon. It was a game similar to the one enjoyed by Linton Gaetz in the late 1800s. Decades later, Marjorie's brother, Harold, would build toys and demonstrate the hoop game for still another generation of Dyers.

In the late 1940s, Harold made the hoop game and another very special toy for his young son, Alvin. An unusual marble game, it was built from a wooden apple box turned on end. Harold cut down the box until it was about ten to fifteen centimetres (four to six inches) wide. At the top, he bored a hole that fed into a curved track within the box. Both top and bottom had areas for

the marbles to collect. Alvin and his brother had great fun pouring marbles down the hole, and speed was everything. The idea was to create a non-stop stream of marbles, and the racket must have made the walls reverberate.[9]

In the meantime, Marjorie Dyer became a teacher. Her pupils had Christmas concerts, but one of her jobs was not so pleasant. She had to count the gopher tails brought in cans by her students, and some tails were old and "stinky." Nevertheless, endlessly patient boys and girls had waited hours with their snares for the gophers to pop up from their holes. The municipality paid the children a penny for each tail, and Marjorie kept their records. About 10 years earlier, her younger sister and brother had climbed trees on their way to school, collecting crows' eggs and netting a penny or two per egg from the municipality.

Here, the child at the right stands on small stilts. The impressive stilts of the other two children appear to be made of poplar.

Provincial Archives of Alberta A 5917

36

Through the Eyes of Children

Of course, play wasn't always a laugh a minute. Children's feelings were hurt because they were chosen last for a team. Boys returned to school with bloody noses or bruises from lunchtime accidents, roughhousing, or fights. Boys, more often than girls, received the strap for being bad apples in the schoolyard. Parents scolded children for clomping around in muddy boots, shoes, and clothes. Children envied playmates who had more or better toys. Some were the brunt of teasing. A child with highly unique interests might have only a very few playmates, let alone soulmates, in a small school.

Conditions were not always perfect for play. Floods plagued southern Manitoba in the spring of 1950, but Marjorie and Betty Malofie braved the waters for their swing, made of rope and a piece of board and hung from a big tree. Provincial Archives of Manitoba, Andrew Malofie Collection, 118

Play could turn to tragedy. In her autobiography *Never Borrow Trouble*, Ignatia Lanigan Grams tells of the wonderful Farmers' Picnics held at a lake near Wilkie, Saskatchewan. One Sunday, a boy died. Standing on the dock, he dived into the lake in a spot that was too shallow, broke his neck, and drowned. Just when Ignatia and her family arrived, rescuers were bringing his body from the water. Don't look, her mother said, "but I did because I was curious and scared at the same time." [10]

Most farm children had the joy of holding tiny, down-covered chicks in their hands. Each one was a treasure, and the sound of their cheeps was more exciting than music and rhymes. With its heater to keep the chicks warm at night, the brooder house was stifling, but it was still fun to watch the chicks scurry beneath the hood.

Whether purchased from a hatchery or hatched by a setting hen, chicks were the highlight of spring for many farm children.
Provincial Archives of Manitoba, Jessop Collection 92, N3140

Some mornings, the brooder house was a sad place, though. A chick—sometimes many chicks—lay dead, smothered by other chicks that huddled too closely together.

Children's emotions were also mixed at Saturday afternoon matinees at the movie house. Most shows were upbeat and filled with action, and actors such as Hoot Gibson and Tim Maynard portrayed cowboys. Later, Roy Rogers and Zorro kept kids spellbound. Bambi was even more wonderful than the wild deer these farm kids had seen at home. Every silver-screen "bad guy" seemed magnified and so did the tragedies. A concerned parent might even remove a child and wait in the theatre vestibule until a sad or scary part was over.

Christmas was different in those days. Children received fewer presents and found more pleasure in one apple or orange, nuts, or hard candies. Gwyneth Whilsmith, who grew up in the 1930s near Brock, Saskatchewan, remembers her favourite gift: a book. She also has fond Christmas memories of playing family games, such as poor pussy. As a blindfolded pussycat, Uncle Art would crawl from one chair to the next, guessing who sat in each chair, based only on how the player stroked his head and commiserated, calling "poor pussy" in strange voices. Uncle Art's laughter kept the children in stitches, and that memory remained far more vivid than any gift for Gwyneth.

Even in the poverty-stricken, drought-cursed, grasshopper-infested prairie of the Dirty Thirties, the land itself provided wonderful entertainment for children. They could watch field mice, beavers, muskrats, prairie chickens, ducks, crows,

magpies, and porcupines—but keep the dog away from the quills—and they could search for nests. For children, nothing was too small or insignificant to be the source of wonder or amusement. Born in 1924, Harold Draper was the son of English parents who settled at Lenore, Manitoba. He and his friends collected grasshoppers of different colours.

In this photo, Robert Carson of Edmonton, Alberta, sits on his front porch and uses 3–D toy glasses to read a comic. Early popular comic books included Betty and Veronica (1940s), Loveland (1940s), Superman (1938), and Donald Duck (1939).
City of Edmonton Archives EA 597-6

Rosalee van Stelten, of Dutch heritage, grew up on Valour Road in Winnipeg, Manitoba. Like most kids, she played marbles and, of course, there were many marble variations. Some child always wanted to win another's steelie, a special marble that had originated as a machine's ball bearing.

In her boyfriend's backyard, Rosalee re-enacted Tarzan movies. And although most householders caught flies on long, sticky tapes,

In the 1920s, these southern Alberta children were interested in tadpoles. Others collected bugs, butterflies, stamps, rocks, comics, and hockey cards.
Glenbow Archives NA 2540–6

final blow. Was it the thrill of the kill that kept us going? The excitement of the chase? The trophy pile of tiny corpses we counted after each day's sortie? (Bluebottles were prized the most, for their evasive action and colour.) Was it altruism: reducing the plague of pesky disease carriers? Whatever the motive, I can still feel the rush of adrenaline, hear the excited cries wafting through time and space: "Emergency case!" [11]

Rosalee and her friends liked to hunt them down in person. Best friend Donna had a real flyswatter, but the other children used rolled-up newspapers:

In Donna's backyard, slung on a pair of sawhorses, was an old wooden door, which we used as a mortuary ... We were not cruel to our prey but strived for the quick flick of the wrist, which meant instant death. If our strike merely wounded the target, we shouted "Emergency case!" and Donna rushed to our aid to deal the

Prairie children also delighted in picking wild plants, such as crocuses, pussywillows, tiger lilies, wild roses, buttercups, shooting stars, and especially dandelions. The long stems of dandelions could be linked to make necklaces, bracelets, and headbands. Once dandelions had gone to seed, what child didn't love blowing the fluffy seed parachutes far and wide!

Flowers could also magically divine the true feelings of boyfriends. As a girl plucked off each petal, she would say, in alternation, "He loves me, he loves me not." Whichever phrase coincided with the last petal would be true, so the game would end with a smug, joyful grin or with disdain for silly superstitions.

Hanging around with friends and family, such as these children of the Ewelme Hutterite Colony in southern Alberta, was sometimes the best fun— no matter what the cultural heritage or decade. Glenbow Archives NA 1079-2

Eventually, programs such as "The Happy Gang" and "The Shadow" became popular, but childhood games and pastimes didn't change much until the 1950s. Then television cast its eerie glow across prairie living-rooms. By the mid-1960s, those black-and-white images from around the globe began to change childhood in the West. Rather than read comics, children watched *Rin-Tin-Tin*, *Leave It to Beaver*, and *Donald Duck* cartoons. After the Second World War, plastics became common

Spear grass made a good tooth-pick. Wheat provided chewable gum. The calyx of yellow caragana flowers tasted sweet, and the seed pods were fun to pop. Rose hips and saskatoons belonged in every playhouse cupboard. Children's socks and their companionable dog were covered with burrs that had to be removed one by one. Even a pile of dirt could be fun if trans-formed into a roadway for toy cars and trucks.

By the 1920s, radio brought the world into some prairie homes.

At Davidson, Saskatchewan, Doug Drew and the Miller brothers built their own go-cart. Finding parts such as a steering wheel and tires was seldom easy, but go-carts were fun even before they were finished.
Saskatchewan Archives Board, R-A 20229

At this Legion picnic at Morrin, Alberta, in 1957, both boys and girls ran the wheelbarrow race. Thirty years earlier, girls running the race would have been unthinkable.

Glenbow Archives NA 2262-15

expected to put in twelve years at school, let alone mastering anything equivalent to the computer. Children didn't dash from a judo drill to their appointment with the math tutor while eating a fast-food supper in the car. They weren't bombarded with the tidal wave of information and choices that swamp kids today.

At the same time, their lives were complicated in their own ways, especially on farms. Pigs had to be slopped, cows milked, cream separated, butter churned, eggs gathered, gardens weeded, corn husked, peas shelled, potatoes dug, raspberries picked, jars of pickles fetched from the root cellar, flies swatted, floors mopped, younger siblings babysat, wood chopped, and clothes hung out to dry. Children did all this and more: they picked rocks out of the fields, they lugged sealers of water to the threshing crew, and they kept an eye on Grandma

and cereal companies began including small toys, such as cars, in boxes. Bicycles and hula-hoops, Halloween parties, and pyjama parties were also common. Parents could buy ice cream, candy, and cookies, and kids could collect baseball cards from bubble gum. Eventually, even television lost some ground when computers brought a new world into the home.

People reminisce about "the old days" as a simpler time. Back then, fewer kids were

while Mother chopped the head off a chicken, plucked its feathers, and gutted it so she could roast it for supper.

There was just a ton of manual labour in a rural home—too many jobs for the parents to handle alone. As well, a school bus didn't deliver children to and fro; they had to get to school on horseback or on their own two, often poorly clad, feet. No doubt children were often exhausted. And if they hankered for a new toy or game, they might have to earn the money for it by doing odd jobs for someone else.

A child who had no chores—perhaps the baby of the family—might glance around the homestead and see nothing with a hint of

In 1969, these Calgary, Alberta, boys played leapfrog along the sidewalk. A child in a toy car is visible between the legs of the standing boy. Hopscotch is another activity that has stood the test of time, especially for girls. When there wasn't a sidewalk, children drew the pattern in the dirt.
Glenbow Archives, Calgary Herald Collection, Children, File 3, 28 July 1969

fun except for one old, tired-out teddy bear. Yet he wouldn't dare complain of boredom, for fear Mother would find a chore for him to do. So he'd wander outside, whistle for the dog, and seek out something to occupy himself, maybe look for frogs, check on the latest batch of kittens, or even walk to town to buy a nickel's worth of gum, chewing and snapping it on the store's front step with a couple of pals.

Yes, childhood's setting has changed dramatically since then, and yet children haven't changed at all. They still thrive on, and depend on, joy, laughter, and good times. It's as important a daily requirement for today's youngsters as it was years ago.

Notes

1. E.A. Corbett and A.W. Rasporich (Editors), *Winter Sports in the West*. Calgary, AB: Historical Society of Alberta, 1990, 16–37.

2. Leonard Linton Gaetz, *The Family Story*. Calgary, AB: no publisher given, 1978, 485–486.

3. Georgina Thomson, "Children Enjoyed Life on Pioneer Homestead" [*Calgary Herald*], no date given, Glenbow Library, Clipping File, Frontier and Pioneer Life.

4. Millicent Banner Hansen, taped telephone interview with the author, 20 May 1999.

5. Edith Young Vereshagin, taped conference call including Audrey Young Smith and the author, 26 May 1999.

6. Henry (Nibs) Akers, taped telephone interview with the author, 28 May 1999.

7. Ellen Cole Biette, taped telephone interview with the author, 3 June 1999.

8. Marjorie Dyer Kross, taped interview with the author, 1 June 1999.

9. Alvin Dyer, based on conversations with the author, 20 April 1999, 8 June 1999.

10. Ignatia Lanigan Grams, *Never Borrow Trouble*. Prince George, BC: I. L. Grams and Tabor Publishing, c. 1995.

11. Rosalee van Stelten, letter to the author, 4 May 1999.

DEDICATION

With love to my grandson Jeremy, so you can learn how things were, and to the Lamden family, especially Patti, with whom I shared so many good times in my own childhood.

ACKNOWLEDGEMENTS

Special thanks to Ellen Biette, Henry (Nibs) Akers, Millicent Hansen, Audrey Smith, Edith Vereshagin, Marjorie Cross, Alvin Dyer, Patti Forest, and the Charyk family.

Select Bibliography

Baerg, Harry. *Prairie Boy*. Washington, DC: Review and Herald Publishing Association, 1980.

Broad, Laura Peabody and Nancy Towner Butterworth. *The Playgroup Handbook*. New York, NY: St. Martin's Press, 1974, 1991.

Corbett, E.A. and A.W. Rasporich. *Winter Sports in the West*. Calgary, AB: Historical Society of Alberta, 1990.

Coutts, Edward. *Meanderings of a Parson's Son*. Toronto, ON: Palmerston Press, 1986.

Drake, Jane and Ann Love. *The Kids Cottage Games Book*. Toronto, ON: Kids Can Press, 1998.

Draper, Harold. *Growing Up in Manitoba*. Regina, SK: Canadian Plains Research Centre, 1998.

Gaetz, Linton Leonard. *The Family Story*. Calgary, AB: no publisher given, 1978.

Grams, Ignatia Lanigan. *Never Borrow Trouble*. Prince George, BC: I.L. Grams and Tabor Publishing, c. 1995.

Gray, James. *The Boy from Winnipeg*. Toronto, ON: Macmillan of Canada, 1970.

Hamilton, Zachary Macaulay and Marie Albina Hamilton. *These Are the Prairies*. Regina, SK & Toronto, ON: School Aids and Text Book Publishing Co., Ltd., c. 1948.

Hofer, Samuel. *Born Hutterite*. Saskatoon, SK: Hofer Publishers, 1991.

Miller, Bettina (Editor). *We Made Our Own Fun*. Greendale, WI: Reminisce Books, Reiman Publications, 1995.

Stegner, Wallace. *Wolf Willow*. New York, NY: The Viking Press, 1955. Compass Books Edition, 1966.

Thomson, Georgina. "Children Enjoyed Life On Pioneer Homestead," [*Calgary Herald*], no date given. Glenbow Library, Clipping File, Frontier and Pioneer Life.

Wetherell, Donald and Irene Kmet. *Useful Pleasures*. Regina, SK: Alberta Culture and Multiculturalism and Canadian Plains Research Centre, 1990.

Whilsmith, Gwyneth. *Hear the Pennies Dropping*. Goderich, ON: Gunbyfield Publishing, 1987.

Young People of All Ages: Sports, Schools and Youth Groups in Calgary. Calgary, AB: Century Calgary Publications, 1975.

Winnipeg Free Press, 19 February 1966; 13 July 1978; 1 September 1983; *Winnipeg Free Press Tribune*, 4 October 1958; 18 April 1970; 19 February 1977; 18 May 1977; 12 May 1979; *Tribune Focus*, 18 April 1970, 20 July 1974.

The Western Producer, 21 June 1973.

Trade Catalogues

Hudson's Bay Company, Autumn and Winter Catalogue, 1910–1911. Reprint by Watson & Dwyer Publishing Ltd., Winnipeg, MB, 1977.

Montgomery Ward & Co., Spring and Summer Catalogue, 1895. Reprint by Dover Publications, New York, NY, 1969.

Sears, Roebuck and Co. Catalogue, 1902. Reprint by Gramercy Books, New York, NY, 1993.

T. Eaton and Company Ltd. Catalogue, 1888–1889.

T. Eaton Company Ltd., Spring and Summer Catalogue, 1897.

T. Eaton Company, Ltd. Catalogue 1901. Reprint by Musson Book Company, Toronto, ON, 1970.

Interviews

Akers, Henry (Nibs). Taped telephone interview with the author, 28 May 1999.

Biette, Ellen Cole. Taped telephone interview with the author, 3 June 1999.

Hansen, Millicent Banner. Taped telephone interview with the author, 20 May 1999.

Kross, Marjorie Dyer. Taped interview with the author, 1 June 1999.

Smith, Audrey Young and Edith Young Vereshagin. Taped conference call, 26 May 1999.

Front cover photo courtesy the John Charyk Collection, Charyk family.

Back cover image courtesy Saskatchewan Archives Board R–A 18863–3

Image, page i, courtesy Provincial Archives of Manitoba, L.B. Foote Collection, 1337

Cover and interior design by Brian Smith / Articulate Eye

We acknowledge the support of The Canada Council for the Arts for our publishing program.

We acknowledge the financial support of the Government of Canada through the Book Publishing Industry Development Program for our publishing activities.

Printed in Canada

99 00 01 02 03 / 5 4 3 2 1

CANADIAN CATALOGUING IN PUBLICATION DATA

Reineberg Holt, Faye.
Homemade fun

(Prairie Heritage series)
Includes bibliographical references.
ISBN 1-894004-35-3

1. Games–Prairie Provinces–History. I. Title. II. Series
GV1204.15.R44 1999 790.1'922'09712 C99-910939-1

FIFTH HOUSE LTD.
A Fitzhenry & Whiteside Company
#9 6125 - 11th Street SE
Calgary, AB, Canada T2H 2L6